It's My Life, My Way

Cut the noise and chase your dreams

Kanak Suri

PARTRIDGE
A Penguin Random House Company

To order additional copies of this book, contact
Partridge India
000 800 10062 62
orders.india@partridgepublishing.com

www.partridgepublishing.com/india

Dedicated to every teenager.

आनन्द शर्मा, सांसद
ANAND SHARMA
MEMBER OF PARLIAMENT
(RAJYA SABHA)

सत्यमेव जयते

28, Lodhi Estate
New Delhi-110003
2nd November, 2014

Dear Kanak

Congratulations for putting your thoughts together in your book- "**it's my life, my way**" which makes an interesting reading. The book provides a fresh perspective as teenage is all about being enthusiastic, joyful and ambitious.

Life for many brings happiness, joy and success and sometimes sorrows and setbacks. It's therefore important not to get overwhelmed in challenging situations and remain resolute to overcome hurdles. Teenagers and for that matter, all people, need to nurture a competitive spirit, think big, and make it one's life endeavor to realize the dreams.

Both acceptance and gratitude give a person inner peace and help in remaining connected to reality and our surroundings. Teenagers by nature are aspirational, inquisitive and impatient. We surely need to keep positive attribute as one evolves to grow. Young people in teenage are on the threshold of life as they embrace the world where both challenges and opportunities beckons them. Irrespective of one's achievements, wealth and standing in the society, humility and compassion towards fellow human being is always uplifting.

The book is analytically insightful about a teenagers mind, anxieties and expectations. To remain positive and focused, helps in realizing hopes and aspirations. Your book will help readers to reflect, remain motivated and ready to accept changes which, are integral in the journey of every human being: young and old.

My best wishes to you for sharing with us your perspective of what you rightly describe an amazing life.

All the Best!

Anand Sharma

Ms. Kanak Suri,
New Delhi

Ph. : 011-24634755 Telefax : 011-24643663 E-mail : anandsharma@sansad.nic.in

Acknowledgements

This book has been a dream, a dream of changing the lives of many teenagers. Before I can thank anyone, I would like to thank God for making this dream a reality and for making this happen.

First and foremost, I would like to thank Rhonda Byrne, the author of The Secret, who has deeply inspired me. Rhonda Byrne, thank you for changing my life so that I could change others'.

Next to thank is my father (Sushil Suri), who is the gem of my life. I won't be able to fully thank you ever, Dad.

Mom (Anju Suri) and sister (Aanchal Di) for being the greatest pillars of support. Thank you for all that you do for me.

Thanks to my adorable little brother, Arjun and to my sisters who are ready to do anything for me and who bring the happiness and energy in my life. Thanks to Arjun for specially making the cover.

Special thanks to my family members, each one of you, from the youngest to the oldest. You guys have made me what I am today with all your love, support and appreciation. I'm blessed to born in such a family.

Another special thanks to all my friends for standing by me, for making me happy and for giving me amazing memories. You made my life so much easier and better.

Thanks to all the amazing people whom I met at LBW who totally made it the best experience of my life. I learnt so much from each one of you!

Thanks to my publishers, who have done so much for me to bring the book to the stage where it is today.

Thanks to Vandana Ma'am for teaching me all those things, which no one ever did. You gave me a new life.

Thanks to Shiamak Davar's Institute for the Performing Arts for being the greatest dance institute and for giving me the gift of dance. Thanks to all the instructors who taught me from my first batch to my last batch.

Lastly, thanks to all the teachers of the Modern School Vasant Vihar New Delhi, for guiding me, supporting me and for giving me excellent education and skills.

If I missed somebody, please forgive me. Thank you so much, everyone. I love you all always.

Kanak Suri

Preface

I have had a fascination for writing since the last few years and was writing small notes and quotes about life.

I am known in the family for posting long messages on our WhatsApp family group.

I've always wondered if there is something more to life than what we teens go through. I always thought that the teens are very confused and, to an extent, frustrated from the day-to-day issues even though they have big dreams in front of them.

As a group of friends, we once made a project called Teen Trauma; it could not get the approval of the selection committee, but the things were hanging at the back of my mind.

I am a very positive person thanks to the movie called The Secret produced by Rhonda Byrne. I could connect the chord with myself and get a fair idea of what was going on in my life.

I kept writing my notes in my diary, which nobody could read. Then one day, I decided that I would write a book with all the ideas and thoughts which I have learned and perhaps not every teen is fully aware and clear about.

Here you are holding the book It's My Life, My Way in your hand.

Kanak Suri

Contents

*It's My Life,
My Way*

Introduction

It's my life, my way

The teenager – a young prolific mind.

Teen-age is the tender age full of happiness, desires, and joy, but is also full of problems, sadness, and complaints. As one enters the teenage years, one has demands and expectations, which are followed by criticism and curiosity.

Teenage life is about socializing, interacting with others, and exploring yourself. It's about chasing your dreams, but also there is a lot of peer pressure and parents' expectations.

There is a lot that goes on in the mind of a teenager who is busy on the gadgets the whole day. But there are volumes of books, studies, coaching, exams, and the peer pressure.

There are lots of unanswered questions which pop up every day in these young minds. Not many people know that so many teenagers sleep with a sigh but forget to wake up with a ray of hope.

I have written this book especially for growing teenagers. This book is not an autobiography. This book is every teenager's account. It is a self-help book for every teenager who wishes to reach great heights in life but is somehow stuck somewhere.

Being a teenager myself, I understand the situation of others like me. I understand what we go through and where we want to go. I have listed some simple tips which I came across through my experience for you to make your lives amazing.

The motive of this book is to tell my friends about the simple things which I learned that can have a huge impact on the way they live their lives. It is not to tell them about big philosophies but to give them simple tips in a friendly manner.

It is to make them realize that their lives will always be a perfect blend of opposites. It is for them to happily live each moment of their lives despite its ups and downs. My main goal is to end the long-lasting cycle of blames and criticism and to see happy individuals.

Another objective of this book is to see teenagers reaching great heights and achieving their goals despite the problems they face. It is to make them accept the problems and challenges that come their way and move ahead with them.

I want to give new and easy ways to teenagers to get out of the teenage trauma and make them cut the noise and focus on their targets.

The most important aspect of the book is the action. The motives behind me writing the book can only be successful if the reader jumps into action; otherwise, it's just a nice book.

The book is titled It's My Life, My Way because that is what every teenager thinks: 'It is my life, and I want to live it my way.' Agreed. The thought process is right, but is it leading anywhere?

It is for the teenager to decide if he or she wants to change his or her ways for a better life or not. If the teenager does not wish to change his or her ways, reading the book is pointless for him or her.

The choice is in the reader's hands. Awesome things are knocking on the door; he or she has to decide whether to open the door or not.

The topics that I have listed in the book are topics that teenagers come across every day in their lives—for example, happiness, desires, passion, problems, acceptance, thoughts, and love.
I have purposely begun each chapter with a problem and ended each chapter with the solution. The problems highlighted in the beginning of each chapter are just few of the instances that I have seen, heard, and experienced in my circle. But there are hundreds of things like these that developing teens go through.

The examples given in the book are very general in nature and do not necessarily represent a particular class or group of people, but I have tried to cover a typical young high school kid who wants to fly high but has crippled his wings.

Each chapter that follows talks about how you should change your ways about a particular area in your life in order to move towards a fantastic life.

I always want to see everyone happy and living happy lives. This book is only a small step that I wish to take for the society. If I can improve the lives of even some teenagers, my purpose of writing this book will be successful.

I would like to say to all teenagers:

'Come. Step in, and let the miracle begin.'

It's my life, my way.

It's my Life and
I am Happy

Chapter 1

It's my life. Am I really happy?

'It's my life. I want to zoom around with happiness, but there are so many issues.'

'I have so much negative stuff around me, and one day I want to leave everything and just be alone.'

'I want to live my life the way I want, but I can't do much about it.'

Yes friends, no need to worry. This is what I hear from most of my fellow teens I have met.

In today's competitive world, you all are struggling to find happiness, but at the back of your minds, you know that you are far away from it.

Many of the young teens think they are not happy. Look at this:

'I was born in a good family, I go to a good school, I have good friends, and my life is okay. I almost get everything that I need. I eat good food and have plenty of clothes, but am I really happy?'

'I sleep really late every night after talking to my friends, but I have to get up every day at 6.30 a.m. There is a lot of work to do in the school and then the homework. My friends are my only entertainment in school. I have a good time in school, but am I really happy?'

'I come back home and have to go for extra classes. Well, on weekends I somehow get to go out for dinner, but that's like once a month. Sometimes I get time too for sports or activity classes. I get to enjoy sometimes, but am I really happy?'

'I want to become a writer or musician or cricketer, but I know I'll eventually be doing my dad's business. My siblings keep annoying me, and we end up having arguments every time. Still, in front of my parents, I try to remain calm, but am I really happy?'

'I get to go for a vacation once or twice a year, and that too after a lot of adjustments in extra tuitions and my swimming classes. I go for parties sometimes and always look forward to these happy moments, but am I really happy?'

This is the story of almost all teenagers; all teens go through the same issues. So let's start working on how to get out of this situation and be happy.

Welcome to - It's my life, my way

Happy. Are you really happy, or are you just superficially happy?

Do you really love everything in your life, from your old car to your books? Do you wake up every day with a smile on your face and thank God before you sleep after a beautiful day?

Do you pretend happiness, give fake smiles the whole day, and are more frustrated at the end of the day?

Are you really happy? The obvious answer is no!

Now, let's come to the main point and start working for the solution.

What do we do now? Before you start changing anything in your life, the first thing you need to do is to be happy, actually happy. This is a good beginning.

When you're really happy, you feel like jumping every day. That's when every day is like an exciting journey.

That's when you walk to school with a lot of enthusiasm and reach back home and hug your mother with excitement and joy.

The fact is that we all feel that we're happy and we display we're happy and never admit when we're sad. But if we look deep inside, we'll find many scars hurting us.

Happiness is more than just cracking jokes with your friends or laughing with your family.

Happiness is enjoying the bliss of every moment.

Happiness is enjoying the bliss of every moment.

Happiness is like going for a party and getting gifts every day. Happiness is like a treasure every day and it is inside you. But we keep looking to the outside world for happiness.

Happiness depends upon ourselves. (Aristotle)

You might say, 'Cool, I want to be happy.' But how can you be happy?

Happiness is based on a simple principle: nothing is very hard, too fast, or very complicated; everything is very easy and basic.

Simplicity is the essence of happiness. (Cedric Bledsoe)

I have a simple formula, which I have tried and found that it works very well. You just have to follow the chain of happiness.

The first step is to be happy. Once you're going to be happy, everyone will seem happy to you. Whether or not the people around are happy, you will be as happy as you are.

Also, since you're happy, you'll be able to make others happy, and you'll attract more happy situations, circumstances, and events. You will now be in a happy mode; all your work will start getting done with ease.

Because you'll be feeling good, you'll be doing everything well with all your enthusiasm and energy. Each day will become a beautiful one, and life will become just the way you want it to be.

So that's how this chain of happiness works and why it is a chain—because it's all connected and it keeps on following from one person to another.

It's easy to break the chain of happiness, but it is not so difficult to get it back.

And if you break the chain, your flow of happiness will also break off, and you'll be back to sadness and pain.

It's easy to break the chain of happiness, but it is not so difficult to get it back.

And if you make this happiness chain a daily routine in your life, you're sure to get all that you want.

Happiness is in your hands; you have to be happy to get a happy life.

Now I come to the million-dollar question: how do I become happy in the first place?

'I am ready to follow the chain of happiness, but how do I start the chain if I am so sad and so depressed?'

'How can I be happy if I have so many problems?'

'How can I be happy if everybody is against me?'

'How can I be happy if nobody loves me?'

'How can I be happy if I do not score well?'

The list goes on. There are thousands of reasons to be sad; there is one reason to be happy, and that is to be you.

We all have dreams, and we all want to be happy, but we get lost on the way and get trapped in the 'noise', which creates more confusion. I have heard from many teens, and it is this noise that pollutes their minds and dreams.

In the next few chapters, I have picked up one problem at a time and tried to resolve the same then and there. Chapters may not be in the right sequence of our problems, but I have tried to cover the most common problems we come across.

The problems of us teenagers are more complex than they seem superficially, but the solutions are simple.

Life is waiting for you. So, let us start the journey to Happiness, one step at a time.

It's my life, and I want to be happy

When you are happy, your body releases 'happiness hormones' that makes you happier and then more. Then it spreads all around you. It gives great feelings and great open-minded thoughts, and you want to love the world around you. When happy, you are more adaptable and more accommodating. You are full of energy, and you think of growth and prosperity. It is a chain reaction.

I am ready to
CHANGE

*It's my life and
I am ready to change*

Chapter 2

It's my life, and I am what I am

'It's my life. I am what I am. Why should I change?'

'I want everything in my life to go the way I want. I want others to think like me only.'

'Let me know what do. I don't like changes every time.'

Do these statements sound familiar? Have you heard friends and colleagues talking of the same stuff every now and then?

Bingo! You are on the spot. All teenagers want a beautiful life but are not ready to change. My observation is that most of you are living in your comfort zones and are happily settled there. When something new comes, you react and resist the change.

If you look at the examples that follow, you can make out how common the phenomenon is.

'I'm living a cool life. I'm intelligent, I get good grades, and I hang around with good friends. My life is running very smoothly, so to say. Now somebody comes and wants me to do things in a different way, I do not like it. I am what I am. Why should I change?'

'Everyone tells me that if I do not get good grades, I can never be successful in life. But what if I think I can't do it? Am I ready to change?'

'Some people say I should change my school and go to IB Board, but what about my friends? What will I do without them? Am I ready to change?'

'I want to look slim and trim and really want to join a nice gym, but I do not like getting up in the morning. I hate a fixed routine. Am I ready to change?'

'I want to join the media club in school. I would like to make a mark in public speaking, but I am too shy to go up to the teacher. Am I ready to change?'

It's not easy to accept the change. It hurts, it pushes you back, and also it gives new challenges.

But what choice do we have? We have to change.

Welcome to - It's my life, my way

Yes, my friends, are you ready to move towards the path of success, joy, and happiness?

Are you all pumped up with energy and passion to do something big in your life?

Are you ready to lead the world and make people follow your path?

> **Are you ready to lead the world and make people follow your path?**

Are you ready to make your parents, friends, and family proud?

Are you ready to get your name embossed in the history textbooks, or are you a confused, sad, and depressed teenager who doesn't wish to come out of this negativity?

If, by any chance, you are yet not ready to change your life, I recommend you don't read further. Just relax and enjoy.

Only if you are ready to change and are ready to accept the change, only then shall the book be of any help to you.

Ultimately, it is your life in your hands; you make it or break it.

Your life does not get better by chance. It gets better by change. (Jim Rohn)

Your drive, ambition, and your willpower are the first things you need to get out of this confusion you are going through, and that all you need.

No teenager—as a matter of fact, nobody—in the world is ever ready for a change.

But sooner or later, we need to admit that life changes at every moment.

Everybody wants to change the world, but nobody wants to change. (Wordboner)

As we close our eyes to the previous day, we shut that chapter and turn the page for a new one.

The moment we get up on a new day, we step into a new world. But sooner or later, we need to admit that life changes at every moment.

You might have heard that change is the only constant in the world. It is happening as you are reading this chapter.

Some changes are external to us, and we cannot do much about it. We just need to adapt ourselves to them.

But here I am talking more about the change that we need to make in our lives to change the world around us.

The moment we get up on a new day, we step into a new world.

Be the change you want to see in the world. (Mahatma Gandhi)

While some just happen slowly and steadily, some changes come as a shock and change our lives dramatically.

Some people who have perfect lives don't want these changes to come, and they get so afraid once a change knocks on the door. They are scared to lose their comfort levels; their security antennas go up immediately.

Changes will happen, regardless of who we are, and we shall learn to deal with them.

You never cross the ocean until you have the courage to lose sight of the shore. (Christopher Columbus)

Whether we like it or not, changes shall happen in everyone's lives every now and then.

But let us come to reality that changes will happen regardless of who we are, and we shall learn to deal with them.

Change happens at its own pace; we need to catch up with the pace, or we will be left out.

> Change will not come if we wait for some other person, or some other time. We are the ones we have been waiting for. We are the change we seek. (Barak Obama)

The first thing you need to do is to believe that each change that is happening in your life is happening for a reason.

That reason, you may not know right now, but sooner or later, you will know it in your life. It is for your good only.

You need to believe that there is some power in the universe that is planning all these changes for you based on your karmas (actions)

So changes happen based on what you do! A poor guy doesn't become a billionaire overnight, or a failure doesn't become a topper in one day.

Changes happen slowly and steadily and for your good, for your benefit.

It may not sound that appealing to you at this point in time, but the earlier you realize the benefit of these changes, the faster you shall step into your beautiful world.

Changes happen slowly and steadily and for your good, for your benefit.

Sometimes, we are stuck with old beliefs and have fixed notions. We need to break the cocoon and be ready to fly.

We need to have good karmas and let amazing changes follow. We need to go with the flow.

Some things are not in our control, but are surely based on our karmas, past and present.

So are you ready to jump? It's time for you lovely teenagers to get ready for the change.

It's my life, and I am ready to change.

Change is the basic phenomena of nature. If you are ready to change, then you are in harmony with nature. As human beings, we change, we evolve, and we adapt. Once we change, we are brand-new individuals and can have a fresh start; the past is gone, washed away. We flow like a river, change paths every mile, but keep flowing. That is the beauty of life. If you decide not to change with the times, you will soon have to look for dinosaurs for your company.

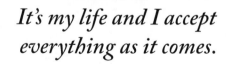

*It's my life and I accept
everything as it comes.*

Chapter 3

It's my life, and I don't get what I want

'I work so hard, do whatever best I can , but I don't get what I want.'

'I can't take no for an answer, and I get frustrated when I don't get what I was working for.'

'I am a very emotional person. I have a small ego, but if I want something, I don't care about anything else.'

I have heard these emotional statements many times over from a variety of teenagers. On the face of it, these look like positive, strong determinations, but these are also the reasons of frustration and disappointment with the teens today in this ambitious world.

All of you have high expectations, and it is good to set your target high, but first you have to learn to accept the things that you have first. If you happen to talk to any of your friends, you will find that most of them are not happy with what you got.

A typical teen story goes like this:

'I live in a good house and get all the good stuff, but I still want to shift into a big bungalow and be as rich as Bill Gates. I am not happy for what I am getting?'

'I'm healthy, tall, and fair, but I still want to lose weight. My friends are skinnier than me. I am not happy for what I am?'

'I come third in the class. That's because there is so much competition. But I keep struggling to come first. I am not happy for what I am getting?'

'I do the dance performances, but I never get a solo. Or I play football but never get to be the scorer. The instructor says other kids are better than me. I am not happy for what I am getting?'

'I had a break-up last week. However, I'm still not over him. I think he's too moody to make up with me. I won't make the effort. He should do it. Why should I bend? I am not happy for what I am getting?'

'I went for a competition last week, and I've been winning it for the last few years. However, a new girl from another school beat me. How can she do that? I'm the best! I am not happy for what I am getting?'

Yes, my friends, that is the most common problem among all ages—more so in teens. You always want more, more, and a little more. At this age, you are never satisfied with what you get. You do not accept what comes in.

Welcome to - It's my life, my way

Step into the world of acceptance, to the greatest achievement one can have—the art of acceptance!

Everything in life happens for good. Acceptance means nothing but coming to terms with life. It simply means catching all the balls that come your way, keeping them aside, and moving on.

Everything in life happens for a good reason.

Life gives you everything; keep accepting whatever comes. Try not to retaliate.

We live in a world of demands and expectations and not acceptance and acknowledgement.

We live in a world of demands and expectations and not acceptance and acknowledgement.

In each day of our lives, we make endless complaints without even realizing it, and we barely accept anything.

> Accept what is, let go of what was, have faith in what will be. (Sonia Ricotti)

We never acknowledge what we have got; rather, we keep fighting for what we haven't got. God has a made a full plan for you, let it unfold.

You have to patiently wait and keep accepting whatever comes now; the best is on the way and will also come to you one day.

Just value all the things that are happening in your life and come to terms with life the way it is.

Learn to accept everyone and everything everywhere.

So, my dear friend, learn to accept everyone and everything everywhere.

We waste lots of time in giving excuses and justifications, and we miss the key point.

> Do not waste your time with explanations, people only hear what they want to hear. (Paulo Coelho)

But, dear teenager, remember that it's better to accept than to expect.

Remember that it's better to accept than to expect. I'm not saying don't expect, do expect, but only once you've learned to accept.

> Hope for the best, expect the worst and take what comes. (Hamilton Crane)

Since you were expecting a 90/90 or an admission to top universities or getting a job in one of the big MNCs, when you don't get that, it is difficult for you to accept what you get.

When you were wishing for a 10 CGPA or a big mansion or a six-digit salary a year and you do not get that, that again makes it difficult for you to accept what you get.

When you are demanding a new phone or camera from your father or more money when you are at the hostel and you do not get that, yet again it is difficult for you to accept what you get.

Dear friend, this is not the case with only you or your friends or your family; it is the case with everybody.

But here I am trying to tell you that you have to accept it because that is a reality. By your not accepting the things, reality is not going to change. If your expectations, wishes, and demands were not fulfilled today, they will be at some other time. But it is important to be Happy. For you to be happy, you have to go with the flow and not against the flow.

> Happiness can exist only in acceptance.
> (George Orwell)

You cannot change the truth, right? You may get a grade of 85/100 this time; it's excellent. You're sure to get a 90/100 next time. Just keep going.

You couldn't get into the top ten universities; you got into the top twenty. Congratulations, it's a great achievement! Work a little harder, and you can do your master's at one of the top ten universities.

Just be ready to face every truth that comes your way. That's is a reality, embrace it.

Perhaps God knows what time what is to be given to you. Just follow the dotted lines.

The people who are not scared of anything that happens in their lives are happy, and are willing to accept everything whatsoever—happily.

If you yourself are more interested in blaming and criticizing others and you do not want to acknowledge and accept the things as they are, then it's really challenging to stay happy.

Whereas, once you've made up your mind that all you want to do is to acknowledge and appreciate things, people and situations, it's very easy. Life will be free-flowing.

Everything is life is delivered to at your doorstep a pre-designed package. It's your, go take it.

So it all depends on you—to accept or to not accept, to like or to dislike, to approve or to disapprove. It's the choice that you make which makes your life beautiful or not so beautiful.

Your reaction to a situation matters more than the action that is outside phenomenon.

You have to accept everything; you have to change your way of looking at life to change your life. In real life, your reaction to a situation matters more than the situation itself.

Even a bundle of roses have some thorns. Even Warren Buffet had sleepless nights. Even Ronaldo gets injuries.

But they all move ahead in life and never stop and count the number of hurdles. They never blame others for the loss.

Thus, once you learn to accept, you learn to live.

It's my life, and I accept everything as it comes.

When you accept everything around you as it comes, the world around you accepts you as you are. You don't have to do any effort for the world to love you, kiss you, and hug you. You will be welcomed everywhere. You are in harmony with the universe, you are in harmony with creation, and more importantly, you are in harmony with yourself.

*It's my life and
I believe in myself.*

Chapter 4

It's my life, and I am not worth it

'It's my life. I have tried everything. It does not work out. I can't do it. For me, it's over.'

'Don't ask me again. I told you, it's not my cup of tea. It's beyond me.'

'People are very smart. I am not worth their friendship.'

Do these remarks ring any bells in your ears? Yes, those are the young teens of today talking. There is a lot of disbelief and self-criticism existing today in this age group.

When you are not getting anywhere, it is easy to blame yourself and hide behind a big wall, and the door closes forever. Many of the young teens sometimes think that they are not worth it.

'My parents say I'm not good enough, that I won't be able to accomplish anything on my own, and that I should simply join father's business. Am I worth it?'

'The tutor did not believe I would score more than 85 per cent. I'm not capable of doing that. Even my friends say the same. Am I worth it?'

'I'm a good singer, but I can't dance that well. My friends laugh at me when I dance. I don't think I can be like Shiamak Davar one day. Am I worth it?'

'I couldn't become the team captain or get into my dream team. I'm really shattered. People just say maybe I didn't deserve it. It demotivates me even more. Am I worth it?'

If you yourself don't believe in you, who else will believe in you, and why should they? Why should people put a stake on you if you are not ready to bet on yourself?

Welcome to – It's my life, my way

Self-pity and self-criticism are the most common beliefs in all the teens. When we want to do something and are not able to achieve success, we get into this negative spiral of self-disbelief.

We see things not as they are, but as we are. (H. M. Tomlinson)

Let me help you understand here that if you have not been able to kiss success, it does not mean you are not competent or you do not deserve it.

You have all the power and magic that is required to be successful. People who have made history did not land from the moon. They were all born like you and me and had gone to the same schools (perhaps not even gone to school) like us.

The difference is that they believed in themselves, they believed that they could do it, and they did it.

The ones who are crazy enough to think that they can change the world, are the ones who do. (Steve Jobs)

One is belief in yourself and your capabilities, and the other is belief in your surroundings, your people, your parents, and your mentors.

Unfortunately, belief and faith are something we have more in others than in ourselves.

It takes a long time to believe in something or someone but only a few seconds to break that belief.

Ultimately, it is self-belief that is going to count in the long run. You should have faith in yourself and your capability. Your imagination is stronger than all the talk around the world.

> It takes a long time to believe in something or someone but only a few seconds to break that belief.

> You can do what you want to do, you can be what you want to be. (David Thomas)

And I'm not talking here about the belief or trust you have in your friend, partner, brother, sister, or parents.

I'm talking about the belief in yourself. All you need to do is believe in yourself and believe that life is going to be beautiful.

> All you need to do is believe in yourself and believe that life is going to be beautiful.

Believe that everything in this world is wonderful despite its ups and downs, and your belief will be there with you, for you, forever and always.

Your belief in yourself should be more than your belief in your partner, mother, brother, sister—anyone. Your belief is going to decide your destiny.

> The only person you are destined to become is the person you decide to be. (Ralph Waldo Emerson)

You don't have to worry whether your belief will be right or wrong because it's yours. You may need to think twice before believing in somebody, but you don't need to do that with yourself.

Just like belief in ourselves, faith is to have full trust on someone or something.

Faith also does not need to be forced on to you; it comes from within and with time.

But sometimes you have faith in some people, and they cheat you. And then you stop having full faith in them ever again.

 It's not that you should not have faith in anyone. You may have faith in your parents or life partners or anyone in your family and even friends for that matter. But if you do not have in yourself, you can't do anything.

Have faith in everybody, but always keep in mind that you are your best friend and not them. If you are in a problem,

I'm sure your loved one will always be there for you, but someone whom you were expecting might just not be there.

Don't break then, and do not expect anything. For you, you matter the most.

And yes, you have faith in Domino's that they'll deliver the pizza in thirty minutes, but you don't have faith in yourself that you can deliver what you plan for yourself.

You have to have unlimited faith in yourself, without fear and doubt. It's your courage and conviction that will matter more than your doubts.

> You have to have unlimited faith in yourself, without fear and doubt.

Belief and faith are very personal and extremely important, extremely beneficial; just add them to your new lifestyle.

It's my life, and I believe in myself.

When you believe in yourself, your whole body, and mind is with you; every part of your body, every cell of your brain is ready to work on your command. When instructions come from you, 100 per cent of you is ready to fire,. That is the power of self-belief. When you believe in yourself, your body language changes, and people see the change; they will start believing in you. They will make others believe in you, and it goes on. It all starts from you.

*It's my life and
I appreciate everything.*

Chapter 5

It's my life, and things are bad

'It's my life. I don't like my friends, I really don't like my new phone, and do ask me about the old laptop which I use. It is very bad.'

'I don't like the morning coffee and the cold sandwiches. The lunch place was horrible. I am hungry, and I feel like kicking somebody.'

'Everything in this room is a mismatch. Want to throw this dresser out of the window.'

I am sure you've heard this stuff in your house last week. It happens everywhere, in every house, and with all the young kids particularly. These are criticisms, complaints, and blames. There is no room for appreciation in this age.

In my discussions with most teens, my observation is that teens do not appreciate the things around them.

Look at some examples below:

'I go to school in a small car. It's a nice car, but the space is too tight and does not have automatic windows, which big cars have. Do I appreciate my car?'

'I got a 90 per cent in my high school. I wanted 95 per cent. I worked so hard for this. This is not fair. Do I appreciate my abilities?'

'My mum gifted me with a new iPhone 4s on my birthday last year. It's a lovely handset, but now everybody carries 5s. I get really pissed off. Do I appreciate my phone?'

'I regularly go shopping every season and on festivals. Still my wardrobe looks empty. I am always short on new dresses. Do I appreciate my dresses?'

'I was elected as the vice captain of the baseball team. I couldn't become the captain. I feel so demotivated. Everyone thought I deserved it. Do I appreciate what I got?'

You love to criticize; you love to find faults. How easy it is to blame others, and you don't need a doctorate degree to find an excuse. Your life is not going to change till you get out of this blame cycle.

Welcome to - It's my life, my way

Have you ever thought about appreciating the things that happen in your life rather than thinking of what goes wrong in your life? Not really, right?

That's because you never thought of appreciating things and looking at their positive side.

We are so busy looking outside for more things that we forget to look inside our bags and in our house for what we already have.

> **Rather than demanding more, you need to learn to appreciate what you already have.**

We all know that for each thing that happens in our lives, there is a positive and a negative aspect. It will always be the perfect blend of both positive and negative.

First, what you need to do is appreciate the positive aspect of each thing that happens in your life. Rather than demanding more, you need to learn to appreciate what you already have.

If you focus on the negative aspect of things, you will not be able to come out of the negativity trap.

You need to positively appreciate all that is happening in your life, irrespective of the fact that you wanted something better.

Appreciation is a wonderful thing; it makes what is excellent in others belong to us as well. (Francois-Marie Arouet)

You have to look at the positive side of everything. Let me explain this with a simple example.

Suppose you went for a conference to somewhere out of town, and your parents spent a lot of money. You put in a lot of hard work to get a prize, but unfortunately, you weren't able to get one.

Now obviously, you will be feeling negative after the conference, and you will not enjoy. You'll spend the rest of the trip thinking that your efforts have gone to waste, and you will feel low.

But very few people will be thinking about the positive aspect of the conference—that you gained so much knowledge and exposure and that you made new friends. So that's the difference between those who look at the positive aspect of each situation and those who look at the negative aspect.

We can't eliminate the negative things, but we can change our way of looking at them and appreciate them.

Even though it is our human nature to generally focus first on the negative aspects and then on the positive one, it's not something we can't change.

We can't eliminate the negative things, but we can change our way of looking at them and appreciate them.

You only need to keep a positive and appreciating approach towards anything that happens in life.

Even if you came fifth in class, just appreciate yourself. Even if you have a small car, just appreciate it.

Learn to appreciate things and people so that they appreciate you. You will see happiness and positivity revolving around you.

Don't get disappointed because you did not get the best thing; just appreciate the fact that you got the second best thing.

Don't cry just because someone else got what you wanted. Just appreciate his efforts and your efforts.

Don't think about why the wrong thing happened; think about the good you can find in what has happened.

Everything happens for a reason. (American proverb)

We all love to criticize others. What do we get out of this?

We all love to criticize others. What do we get out of this? We feel elevated. We feel high by making somebody feel low.

Once you appreciate people and things as they are, people will accept you as you are.

Remember, whatever we give, we receive. If you give criticism, you get criticism back—either from the same source or from any other source.

On the other hand, if you give appreciation, you will get back appreciation either from the same source or any other source.

Whatever we give, we receive.

So it's a cycle. You have to choose whether you want to get into a complex cycle of blames, criticisms, excuses, and explanations or to just simply want to appreciate things as they are.

If you give appreciation, you will get back appreciation—either from the same source or any other source.

Appreciation of your immediate environment takes you closer to your goal, and criticism drags you away from your goal, that's for sure.

Once you appreciate people and things as they are, people will appreciate and accept you as you are.

Simply, without many dos and don'ts, just appreciate things, situations, circumstances, and people around you, and you'll see your life changing. The golden rule to an amazing life is appreciation.

Your friends, teachers, and parents will start seeing you as a positive person, and your life will never be the same again.

So let us get back to work, start appreciating life, and stop finding faults and stop criticizing others.

It's my life, and I appreciate everything.

Two good things happen to you when you keep appreciating everybody and everything. One, it keeps you away from negativity and insulates you from all the negative forces. Second, which is more important, is that once you appreciate something or somebody, you are sending an acknowledgement of what good you have seen. You are placing yourself in that position, and you are anchoring your boat to that position of goodness and beauty. Slowly, you will start seeing appreciation coming back to you in one form or the other.

It's my life and I only discuss solutions.

Chapter 6

It's my life, and I have many problems

'It's my life, but it is full of problems. I can't tell you how I manage my day.'

'It is easy to sit on this home and give a lecture, but you don't know how many problems I have.'

'Problems, problems, and problems all over the place. I cannot take it any more.'

Is this noise looking different than what you hear every day? Sure, you hear the same stuff from all the teens.

My friends, life is full of problems. You have so much to accomplish, and there are so many hurdles on the way.

'I want to do regular practice for volleyball. But I'm not able to go there every day. I don't get time even for my physics class. But what's the solution?'

'I wanted to go for a drum class, but I never got the time from my tuitions. I wanted to make my own band. Now nobody lets me do anything because of my lack of proper training. But what's the solution?'

'I don't have a strong immune system. Even if I eat out one day or get a cold, my temperature starts rising. I get sick almost every month, and now my friends are really tired of all this. But what's the solution?'

'I have to complete school projects and assignments. I somehow manage to get some time on weekends, and that too only after adjusting and skipping a couple of classes. No time to watch news or anything. But what's the solution?'

'I'm very emotional. I tend to get attached to people really soon, but I also develop differences with them really soon if they don't behave with me properly. I become moody and depressed. But what's the solution?'

Yes, problems are all around. Everything is bad, and you are hitting a dead end. So what? What do we do now? We still have to find ways to get out of the problem part and get to the next level.

Welcome to - It's my life, my way

Life is full pf problems and you can go on and keep on talking about the same, but have you ever thought of a solution?

The solution?

'How can I think of a solution, when I have so many problems?'

> **Have you ever thought of solving the problem rather than discussing it more and more?**

Have you ever thought of solving the problem rather than discussing it more and more?

Not really, right? That's okay. This is the part where most of us get stuck—the problems part.

Your problems may be of a different kind, varying from school problems, social problems, relationship problems, financial problems, education problems, and more.

These problems may bother you and disturb your life, but they do have solutions, and the solutions are with you only.

> What lies behind us and what lies before us are tiny matters as compared to what lies within us. (Ralph Waldo Emerson)

It is not possible to have a problem-free life, but it's possible to make sure that you sail smoothly through them.

To every problem, there is a solution, and to every lock, there is a key—but only if you want to find one.

> To every problem there is a solution, and to every lock, there is a key.

There are just a few tips you need to keep in mind the next time you come across a problem.

Firstly, you have to begin with accepting each and every problem in your life, whether big or small, emotional, technical, or anything.

Then you have to keep this golden rule in your head forever: 'Whatever happens, happens for good,' and if there is a bad thing today, then there's definitely a good day stored for tomorrow.

> In the middle of every difficulty lies an opportunity. (Albert Einstein)

Whatever is happening can't be changed, but the way you look at it can be changed.

> **The world is not going to change for you; you have to change to adapt to the world.**

Change yourself; adapt yourself to the situations, circumstances, and events.

The world is not going to change for you; you have to change to adapt to the world.

Okay. How do you begin the change? It starts with changing your thoughts and feelings towards the situations and circumstances and bringing the new feeling that you aren't in any problem any more.

Stop thinking and end your problems. (Lao Tzu)

Many a times, you keep discussing and explaining every little detail of the problem and keep seeking attention from your near and dear ones; I call it sympathy votes.

But these sympathy votes are not going to solve the problem. At best, it can delay the implementation of the solution.

Sometimes you start enjoying the cosiness of the sympathy and feel comfortable and protected in that 'safe' environment, so you do not dare to go out and find solutions.

Never tell your problems to others. 20% don't care and other 80% are glad you have them. (Lou Holtz)

So long as you keep discussing the problems, the problems will keep on increasing, and solutions will not come.

At some stage, you need to shift your focus to the solution part and move all your attention, time, and energy to find solutions.

So long as you keep discussing the problems, the problems will keep on increasing.

Once you start working on the solution, please, please, please, stop discussing the problem again—how deep the problem is, what the issues are, how badly it has impacted you, how bad you feel, etc. Stop all that sad music, and focus on the solution.

Whatsoever the problem may be, however big it may be, you and your thoughts and feelings can help you get over it.

Life is ten percent what happens to you and ninety percent how you respond to it. (John Woodan)

You could do this simply by thinking about the solution and thinking and feeling as if the problem is already solved.

I can't prevent you from thinking and talking about problems, but I can only tell you to shift your focus if you really want to get out of the problem.

One of the suggestions is to just leave your problems aside and focus on other things. One way to forget a problem is to think about something you love the most.

How is that going to help you? Well, since you'll be thinking about the thing you love, you'll be in a happy mood, and you'll forget about the pain and stress the problem brought to you.

Then when you'll be in that happy mode, finding a solution to the problem would be much easier.

Problems cannot be solved with the same of thinking that creates them. (Albert Einstein)

Remember that there is no problem in this world that doesn't have a solution. And there is nothing in this world that happens without a reason or purpose. So keep this thing in mind, and keep moving.

Each thing planned by the universal design will happen. You can only change it by your karmas, thoughts, and feelings before it happens.

Once something has happened, you can't change it, but you can only change your way of seeing it.

Once something has happened, you can't change it, but you can only change your way of seeing it. Accept it, and move forward with it. Believe me, you will feel much lighter.

Also, don't think you can run away from your problems without finding a solution. It will be like running with a forty-kilogram bag on your back.

We all encounter problems every day, and we all find solutions to problems every day.

Small ones get solved, and we forget about them. Sure, the big ones create the little noise. We tend to get panicked when we have to solve the big ones. Bigger challenges are given to you to achieve bigger goals.

Problems are just like the big stones on the path, but the treasure always comes after one crosses them.

> Obstacles are the things a person see when he takes his eye off his goal. (E. Joseph Cossman)

Remember being on a highway and having a diversion? What do you do? You follow the diversion and get back to the expressway in fifteen minutes. That is how life goes on.

You are stuck in traffic, arrive late for the function, and do not get a good seat. That's not the end of world. Life goes on.

Getting ready for the birthday party, you find that your new dress does not fit you. What to do now? Heavens won't fall. Take it easy; there is always a way out.

Problems come, and they distract you; it is their sole purpose—to distract you and perhaps derail you.

> **Problems come, and they distract you; it is their sole purpose.**

Bumps are made on the track for you to fall. You have to focus on your goal and find a way around the bumps.

Challenges are what make life interesting, overcoming them is what makes life meaningful. (Joshua J. Marine)

If you get trapped in a problem, you will end up losing your target line. You have to quickly shift your gears and bring the focus back on the original goal and start finding ways to get out of the present mess.

The whole objective of giving you the problems, whether in a classroom or outside, is to make you more and more strong.

> **Every event, every interaction, every failure is a new learning.**

Once you have handled a problem, once you know how to cross a high bump, your confidence level goes high. Your skill score goes high.

So next time you see a problem, it is an opportunity to increase your skill score. If it's the same old problem which you handled last week, it is not a problem then; you do not get extra marks.

If you handle a new problem—a bigger, different one—your score goes up every time.

That is how we learn in life; every event, every interaction, every failure is a new learning.

Every learning updates our database. We will have answers to so many problems beforehand, and slowly we become experts.

Every problem, situation, and event has a solution. But it may take you the right amount of mental frame to find the solutions. Sometimes, you are lucky, and the answer is right around the corner, but sometimes you may have to move around.

Everybody goes through problems, big or small; that is the story of almost everybody. Sometimes you slow down, sometimes you hit a dead end, and sometimes it makes you rethink your strategy. It's okay so long as you keep a positive frame of mind and you keep moving.

Success is how high you bounce when you hit the bottom. (George Smith Patton)

All said and done, problems come, problems go, and life keeps moving. That is the spirit of the winner.

In three words I can sum up everything I have learned in life, it goes on. (Robert Frost)

Do not ever, ever get stuck because there is a problem. Keep moving, and think creatively to find a solution. That is much easier than going back home and repenting, saying, 'Bad luck, we had a problem', rather say 'Fine, we got a problem to solve'

While we are discussing problems, you might have seen problem people, people who always talk, discuss, and debate problems. And there are others who are solution providers. You know whom to go to.

> Surround yourself with the people who are going to lift you higher. (Oprah Winfrey)

So next time you see a problem, do not get disturbed; embrace the problem and find a smart solution and get over it. Get your score up so that next time it does not hit you below the belt.

It's my life, and I only discuss solutions.

When you face a problem and you take it to the heart, your body withdraws, your arteries shrink, your blood supply and energy go down, and you get a sinking feeling. So the most important thing now is how to get it out. That is the whole game plan; you have to cheat the system and switch the gears and regain yourself back in action. Once you start thinking of solutions, you start fighting back, and in a short time, you come back with a great spirits and action. Once you have surpassed this stage, next time your brain does not take this signal and gives problem a passé. How simple?

*It's my life
and I am passionate.*

Chapter 7

It's my life, but I don't know what to do

'It's my life, but I don't know what to do. I am very confused.'

'It's too early to decide what to do in life. It's time to enjoy. I do not think too much about future.'

'I have so many things in mind. How can I choose one out of them?'

Yes, my friends, there are many more like you who are still confused of what to do in life.

Your uncle meets you at a wedding party and asks, 'Oh great, what are you going to do now? You want to become a doctor?' And of course you are embarrassed; you don't care whether you become a doctor or an engineer.

What are you thinking?

'I have lots of interests, like singing, dancing, and sports. I attend classes for all these. But am I passionate about any of these?'

'Sometimes I think I should be a vet because I like animals, or sometimes I think I should become a designer because drawings interest me. But am I passionate about these things?'

'I like singing in my school band, but I don't think I can do singing all the time. I do it just for fun. But am I passionate about singing?'

'I take art classes because everyone in my family likes art. I don't know if I really enjoy the classes. But am I passionate about arts?'

'Just because everyone in my family is doing business, even I'm told to apply for a graduate degree in business. But am I passionate about business?'

Not to worry, this is a very common problem at this age. We all have so many things that we love and we crave for. But is there something that is very close to your heart?

Are you passionate about any of the things you do?

Welcome to - It's my life, my way

What is passion?

Passion is what you are made of; it is your inner being. It comes naturally to you; it's your natural expression. It is your second skin.

> **Passion is what you are made of; it is your inner being. It comes naturally to you.**

Passion is something which is not a burden for you; it is something for which you don't need to take out time. You do it effortlessly.

Passion is something that you love the most and is a source of happiness for you.

> Success is not a result of spontaneous combustion, you must set yourself on fire. (Arnold Glasow)

Each person has his or her own passion, and that passion can be for anything—dance, music, drama, writing, singing, flying, teaching, sports, or any other thing.

It could be as little as collecting stamps from different countries or as big as being passionate about space labs and undersea explorations.

Your passion need not necessarily be something approved by the society, whether you love to play cricket or love to track million-dollar deals.

You are you. Now isn't that pleasant? (Dr Seuss)

Passion does not have to be created. It's there; you need to explore it. It does not have to be forcefully built into you, and it comes from within.

Don't think that your parents are going to decide your passion for you based on what they want you to do; you have to do it.

Passion does not have to be created. It's there; you need to explore it.

When writing the story of your life, don't let anybody else hold the pen. (Harley Davidson)

You may ask me, 'I love to make nice brownies. Is it my passion?' How would anybody know what your passion is?

Honestly, if you a have passion, you know it.

What is it that gives you a kick? What is it that wakes you up from the bed?

What is it that drives you crazy? It comes naturally to you; you do not have to think twice.

Like for me, my passion is dance. And why dance? Because dance is something that I have loved more than anything else and because if I have two things to choose from, dance is always my first choice even if the other option is my studies. I do not have to do any effort for that.

Passion can make you touch greater heights in life, provided you follow it to the end.

Other people's opinion should not stop you from pursuing your passion.

Do not let what other people think stop you from doing things you love. (Unknown)

Passion can make you touch greater heights in life, provided you follow it to the end.

If you are lucky and your passion becomes your profession, you'll have the most successful life ever.

You may have questions like 'Can my passion even earn me enough money? Will I be as famous as I want to?'

Allow your passion to become your purpose and it will
one day become your profession. (Gabrielle Bernstein)

Definitely, it will because that's the thing you're going to do
with so much dedication that success will follow you even
if it's the smallest job.

On the other hand, if you'll be doing something just for the
heck of doing it, you'll be running after success. In that case,
you'll not be able to love that thing as much as you love your
passion, and you'll be surrounded by guilt and regret.

Think again, what makes you get out of the bed ?

Once you've found your passion, then you need to have the
drive to achieve your goals
with your passion however
difficult it may be.

You can't be passionate
about music and doing
nothing about it.

If you are passionate about
music, you can't be sitting at home and doing nothing
about it.

To fulfil your passion, you need to have the energy and
determination. You need to work hard and be ambitious
to achieve your goals. You have to put your 100 per cent to
achieve your goals.

If you are pursuing something that you love, life will be very
smooth, and you can climb the ladders of success pretty fast.

My friends, what your passion can do for you may be something that your parents, even a brother or sister, and for that matter, even your best friend cannot do for you. But passion surely can.

> Light yourself on fire with passion and people will come from miles to watch you burn. (John Wesley)

Your passion can change your mood in seconds. It can bring that smile on your face again, and it will make you fly again.

Now go, explore yourself, and find your passion. And let your passion do miracles.

It's my life, and I am passionate.

When you are passionate, you are singing the song of your soul, and you are dancing to the tunes of your heart. You resonate to the tunes of the universe. Every cell in your body is excited and elevated once you are on your own frequency. When you log in to your passion, your internal unique code, you log in to the universal network, and the whole creation will be there to help support you and love you because this is what you are made for.

*It's my life
and I feel good.*

Chapter 8

It's my life, but I am depressed

'It's my life, but I don't feel good about it. I feel like getting out of this place.'

'It's very boring and depressing these days, really frustrating. Give me a break.'

'Don't expect me to smile now. I am done. Had a bad day. It's crazy.'

Can you tell me how often it happens with you or to somebody around you?

Very often, of course.

Now we are hitting the nail on the head. This feeling good or feeling bad is the main story of your life. This is the main cause of your worry or happiness.

Most of the time, most of the people don't feel good and are rather on the other side of the river, but they expect miracles to happen in their lives. How do you expect anybody to make you happy if you yourself are making yourself sad?

It all starts from you. Look at how young teens feel and still they expect nice, great lives.

'People say I'm moody, I get depressed really soon or suddenly get really happy. I have too many ups and downs. Do I really feel good?'

'It's a nice morning. I woke up late and had brunch. But now my mum's telling me to do my school homework. Do I really feel good on Sundays?'
'I go for dance classes every week. Sometimes it's so tough for me to manage the dance classes with my tuitions. Do I really feel good while dancing?'

'I like cooking at home for fun, but that doesn't mean I want to pursue it as a part of my career. Cooking and culinary classes are too much of a burden for me. Do I really feel good while cooking?'

Feeling low, feeling depressed, and feeling like doing anything is the most common problem among teens. We all go through the same, at one time or another.

But, my friends, this is the most important and vital part of life that has to be addressed as quickly as possible. If you are depressed and don't feel like doing anything, the game is over. You have to come out of this negative feelings quickly.

Welcome to - It's my life, my way

Do you really feel good? Are you really charged up?

Or are you depressed?

Your thoughts and feelings create your life and can even change your life whether for the good or bad as you may like.

Your thoughts and feelings create your life and can even change your life.

What you think about every day and how you feel every day matters a lot in your life.

Attitude is little thing that makes a big difference.
(Winston Churchill)

It is an established process that you get what you think and feel about the most and that you also become what you think and feel about the most.

It is all connected. You think, you feel, you love, and you get what you want.

The universe says, 'Like attracts like.' If you think good and feel good, then you get something good. However, if you think bad and feel bad, then you get something bad in return.

If you say 'I am feeling sad, low, and depressed today,' then you're surely going to attract low people, depressing situations, and bad events.

But if you understand that feeling negative is only going to attract more negativity to your life and then you decide to change your thoughts and feelings, then your life can change in no time.

When I get sad, I stop being sad and be awesome again. (Barney Stinson)

The moment you start feeling good and thinking about all the good things, like happiness, joy, love, and enthusiasm, you will start getting all these things in your life. It all starts with how you feel today.

> Nothing to be rated higher than the value of today.
> (Johan Wolfgang von Goethe)

You can get all that you want in your life just by feeling good about it, thinking about it, and loving it.

So if you really want something but you are not giving positive thoughts and feelings about it, then you are never going to get it.

But on the other hand, if you are really thinking about the things, person, or event and giving out positive feelings about it, then you're moving in the right direction.

> Remember; what goes around, comes around.
> (Unknown)

Moreover, once good things start coming to your life, they start multiplying. You start getting more of happiness, joy, enthusiasm, and the other things that you want in your life.

 There are lots of examples of people from different fields that can tell you how thinking and feeling about good things have brought them immense success.

Virat Kohli plays cricket because playing cricket makes him feel good. Then he keeps thinking about cricket all the time and wishes to achieve great success in cricket. With his hard work and efforts and positive thinking, he has stolen the hearts of many and become a youth icon.

The same goes for Madhuri Dixit when she's dancing or acting, for Bruno Mars when he's singing, or for any model when she's walking the ramp.

Because they think about the thing they love and that makes them feel good, then they start attracting those things into their lives.

On the contrary, if Madhuri had not loved dancing and acting so much, she would never have come back to India and again do what she loves and what makes her feel good.

And let me tell you, if Bruno Mars had not thought about music all the time and if music would have given him negative feelings, then he would never have been such a popular singer.

> Imagination is more important than knowledge. Knowledge is limited, imagination encircles the world.
> (Albert Einstein)

Your feelings make a huge amount of difference—at least, those feelings that go on in your mind most of the time.

But it's not only about thinking; it's about thinking good and about thinking the right things.

> If we keep on thinking about the past, the past will keep haunting us.

If we keep on thinking about the past, the past will keep haunting us. Just leave it. Do not bring it into your story.

Your future is created by what you do today, not tomorrow. (Robert Kiyosaki)

Live in the present, not your past. The past is gone; it's dead. But we keep it alive by remembering it, missing it. Let it go. That's how our feelings control us. We need to control our feelings, not the other way around.

> Live in the present, not your past. The past is gone; it's dead.

Now what do you have to do? Do you continue thinking about the past and wasting your precious time, or do you start thinking about good things in your life that are deciding your future?

With your consistent thoughts and visions, you are actually creating your own future every day.

You are the creator of your destiny. (Unknown)

Sometimes, things don't go the way you want them to go. But that doesn't mean you start having negative thoughts and feelings about them.

In such a situation, you have to change your thoughts and feelings so that you can change the circumstances, events, and situations in your life.

It's very important to understand that the future is very uncertain!

But what is certain is the fact that your future is based on how you are feeling today. Today, you are laying bricks for tomorrow.

Since you want to have a wonderful future, there's one thing you need to know before you go ahead.

Newton's third law of motion: 'Every action has an equal and opposite reaction.'

Newton's third law of motion: 'Every action has an equal and opposite reaction.' This is the basic law that governs our lives, and this has been proven scientifically.

To put it simply, whatever you give, you receive. It's a give-and-take formula—no rocket science. If you give love, you receive love; give hatred, receive hatred; give criticism, receive criticism; and the list goes on.

To tell you how this law matters in the simplest situations of your life to the biggest situations, I'll give you some examples.

It's a give-and-take formula; no rocket science.

Suppose you say thank you to someone, that person will say welcome back at you. Or you say good morning to your teacher, and she will reply back to you. Or even smaller, you smile at somebody,

and that person smiles back at you even if that person is unknown to you.

And let's take it to a bigger scenario. You have to go for a competition or a match, but your day begins on a negative note. Your alarm does not ring or your bathroom does not have hot water or your breakfast has become cold or your uniform is not ironed. You are in a very angry mood.

That's when all your hard work goes down the drain and your whole day goes bad. Because you get what you give— you give negativity (anger, irritation, impatience), and you get back the same.

You will not be able to get any achievement in that event because you were not at all positive. You were surrounded by negativity, and your aura was surrounded by negativity.

So be careful of what you give. Give happiness if you want back happiness, give jealousy if you want back jealousy, lie to other people if you want them to lie to you, and also, help other people if you want them to help you.

Just, think big! Think well! Think positive! Feel good! Feel positive! Feel happy!

And let your thoughts and feelings do miracles for you.

It's my life, and I am feeling good.

When you are feeling good and feeling happy, you get connected to the universe, and you start getting a flow of fresh energy. Your body becomes porous, and you are in a receiving mode. On the contrary, when you are feeling low, depressed, irritated, or angry, you are closing all the pores on your body and stopping all the positive energies flowing into you. Rather, you get a sudden gush of negative forces that surrounds you and makes you more depressed or angry as the case may be.

It's my life and I can fulfill my desires.

Chapter 9

It's my life, and I have many dreams

'It's my life. I have so many desires. I want to become very popular one day.'

'I am not going to be working under somebody my whole of life. I want to set up my own business.'

'I think, dream, and breathe technology. I will build a big technology park when I grow up.'

We all have desires. Dreams and desires are what keep all of us on our toes. But teens today are not sure whether they can really accomplish what is running in their minds or not.

If you believe it, you can do it. If you don't, then sure you won't.

Do the following situations sound familiar to you?

'My dance teacher always gives me solos, and I enjoy dancing a lot. But my mum says I won't be able to make a career in dancing, so I should study. But can I become a successful dancer?'

'Just because everybody in the family is a doctor, even I'm forced to study medical sciences, but I wanted to become a pilot. Can I become a renowned pilot?'

'Public speaking is my strength. I would like to do journalism. But my dad says that I should use these skills in his business company. But can I become a popular journalist?'

'I love playing squash, but everybody says in India only cricketers have a future. Squash is not popular and won't take me anywhere. But can I become the best squash player?'

 'I want to buy a Ferrari. But dad says it's too expensive for him to buy. He says I should earn and then buy it from my own pocket. Can I buy a Ferrari?'

'I want to become a multimillionaire one day. Everyone says it's impossible, I'm not capable, and there is too much competition. But can I become a multimillionaire?'

Your list of desires is endless, but can you fulfil them? What plans do you have to fulfil your dreams?

Welcome to - It's my life, my way

Surely all your dreams can be fulfilled if you're truly passionate about them and truly want them.

> Whatever the mind can conceive and believe, the mind can achieve. (Napoleon Hill)

Now, when they will be fulfilled and how they will be fulfilled, that also depends on you. Most of the people have the problem that they are not clear as to what they want, what they really want.

> First step in getting the things you want from life is this: Decide what you want. (Ben Stein)

Once your goals are clear, you just need to follow some simple steps in order to bring your dreams to reality.
It begins by thinking and dreaming about what you want and not what you don't want.

The second step is for you to believe and really imagine that you've got the thing you are dreaming about.

Now to make your belief come true, just start visualizing that your task has already been accomplished and think how you will feel when it happens.

Take pictures of it and put them on your board or write them in block letters on your board. Then you can see it every day, and then whenever you see it, believe that you have it.

> Imagination is the beginning of creation. You imagine what you desire, you will what you imagine and at last you create what you will. (George Bernard Shaw)

Supposing it's a car that you want; put a picture of it on a board or near your bed so that every time you go to sleep or get up, you see that car and then think about what you will do when it comes—where you will go for a drive, what colour you will buy, who will drive it, and more. Keep doing this every day. And then after some time, your create circumstances to deliver the car you want.

And now, if you want to get good marks, make the report card you want to get.

English	92
Math	100
Science	98
Social Science	97
Economics	90

And then you look at it every day and believe that you've got this report card. Imagine how happy and proud your mother and teachers will be in seeing this report card.

> Dream is not what see in the sleep. Dream is the thing which doesn't let you sleep. (A. P. J. Abdul Kalam)

But at the same time, don't stop studying. You see, you have to study; there is no alternative to that. You have to do your best and believe it also.

Now let me give you another example in my life where I had full faith in myself and was able to use my belief and imagination to reach the goal. I was shortlisted for a position in the Special Potential Batch in my dance institute, and I had an absolute belief that I would get a position.

In spite of the tough competition, I got the recognition just because I believed in myself more than anyone else did in me or more than I did in anyone else.

Whenever you're going for some competition or some big achievements, think about how people will come and congratulate you, how you will respond to them, how happy you will be, and how happy and proud your parents and family will be.

This will get you into achievement mode and make you feel as if you already have it.

And that belief will make you want it even more and will keep your hopes alive, and then all you have to do is continue doing this till the time you get the achievement or success.

And you know what? It's not like you can do it once, and you'll get it! Please don't think like that. And it's not that it takes very long. You can do it every night when you go to bed. First, think about all the things you want and how you're going to feel when you have them.

You can do it in the morning when you're taking a shower. Instead of hearing loud music, you could think about your desires, and then soon you shall get all that you want.

However, some of you may ask, 'Is it all that I need to do to become successful? Can I just lie in bed all day and dream of being successful and will be successful in no time?'

Certainly, that will not happen. All the successful people in the world have worked hard to achieve their goals and believed that they will get them.

Some people want it to happen, some wish it could happen, others make it happen. (Michael Jordan)

The flowers don't blossom without planting a seed, but once the seed is planted, then the gardener has to take care of it, water it, and save it from grazing animals. It will take some time, and only then will it blossom into a beautiful flower and bear a juicy fruit.

Therefore, along with having big desires, you need to have bigger willpower and stronger determination.

As I mentioned in the previous chapter, your hard work, energy, and passion are extremely important. Without them, you can't expect the miracles to happen.

Along with having big desires, you need to have bigger willpower and stronger determination.

You shall get all the success you want, provided you follow the path of hard work and belief.

Also, remember that there is a right time for everything to happen and for you to get some things, so if this doesn't work for you at the first time, don't lose all your hopes.

Defeat is not the worst of failures, not have tried is the true failure. (George E. Woodberry)

You have to keep wishing, keep believing, keep imagining, keep working hard, and keep receiving.

Most importantly, dream big, and dream for the best. You should have only good desires and not evil, nasty desires.

Your dreams and desires can be anything to everything, and you shall get anything whatsoever without any doubts or uncertainties.

Think clearly about your desires, think of every little detail, then get into the feelings of achievement, and stay there while you put all your resources to get to the target.

It's my life, and I can fulfil my desires.

When you think, feel, and visualize your dreams, you place yourself in that frequency, and the message the universe gets from your body and your aura is that of fulfilling of your dreams. Universal energy collaborates everything—all situations, circumstances, and events—in such a manner that you get what you want, provided you remain strongly adhered to your dream and plan and put all your passion, energy, thoughts, and feelings into it.

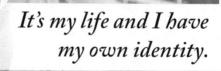

*It's my life and I have
my own identity.*

Chapter 10

It's my life, but I don't know who I am

'It's my life, but I don't have my own identity. I want to become a big man.'

'Dare you talk to me like this? You don't know my father is the mayor of this area.'

'My dad has given me a big car, the latest phone, and what not. But that's not me.'

This is not an uncommon scene whether in big cities or in small towns. You will find all sorts of questions in the young minds these days. While the young teens are moving on a fast track, they are still going through the identity crisis.

While some youngsters may seem happy in enjoying their parents' money, others are worried that this is not what they have created. All teens want to have their signatures on something—something big, something unique.

Look at the following situations:

'My father belongs to an upper-middle-class family, my elder cousins are doing excellent jobs, and everybody asks me about them. But I don't have my own identity.'

'The whole class knows me as the little brother of the school topper and always keeps comparing the two of us. Moreover, I'm even told to follow my sibling's path. But I don't have my own identity.'

'I'm involved in a lot of things—music, football, and academics. People are never able to fully appreciate my potential in any of the things I do. But I don't have my own identity.'

'All my friends bring costly bags and wear expensive belts. Everybody talks about branded clothes and luxury watches. I feel left out. But I don't have my own identity.'

'In today's competitive world, we all are judged by our marks. But sometimes I find more happiness in playing sports than studying, yet I have to study to be in the race. But I don't have my own identity.'

Good beginning. Once we know the problem, there is always the solution. Many youngsters are going through the same struggle and want to leave their footprints on something, something special.

Welcome to - It's my life, my way

Each person is always remembered by his or her own identity. Your identity is what stays in the minds of people forever.

What is your identity? What is your brand?

> If you don't stand for something, you will fall for anything. (Malcolm X)

As teenagers, your identity basically consists of three parts—your family values and upbringing, your passion and skill sets, and most importantly, your relationships with your outer world.

All three have to move in sync. You come from a good, respectable family, but you do not know how to deal with the people. You can see what your identity will be.

You are very passionate about your work, but you don't care for others' needs. You know where you are heading.

Now let us start working on your identity.

Are you a good human being, or are you a bad human being?

Are you a humble and polite human being, or are you a rude, arrogant, and high flyer?

Are you a humble and polite human being? Or are you a rude, arrogant, and spoilt brat?

Do others know you by your good deeds that you do for others, or are you known for hurting others by your actions?

Do you have good moral ethics and values, or are you a disrespectful person with a shady character?

Are you honest and truthful, or you take help of small lies and cheat others?

Your basic character, your morals, your fundamentals are your identity, and that decides your future.

Try not to become a man of success, but a man of value. (Albert Einstein)

Sometimes even the richest people are not known to the world for good reasons because they had a poor character and an unacceptable personality.

And sometimes, even middle-class people become very popular because they have a good and honest character.

There is a very clear line between those who are good, humble and honest or bad, arrogant, and dishonest.

It is for you to decide which side to be on—the right or the wrong.

Howsoever rich or successful you may become, you will always be judged by your karmas and your character first and then by your money.

You will always be judged by your karmas and your character first and then by your money. It's during your teenage years when you start building your character, and if the base is strong, then the structure will survive for long.

You can add more floors to the building anytime on a strong foundation.

Your family values are the basic fabric, and your own identity is the detailed pattern on this fabric.

You should not just be known for what your family does, but also for your own identity.

Sometimes, in order to reach the top, you may wish to take the shortcut. You may reach the top at that time, but sooner or later, you have to pay the price.

> Looking at small advantages prevents great affairs from being accomplished. (Confucius)

All tricks eventually get caught. Sometimes people may manage to earn a lot of money out of them, the punishment they will face later will cost them everything including reputation.

While you are cheating somebody or doing something wrong, you are doing it to yourself.

You cannot cheat anybody except yourself. Your conscience will tell you when you do something wrong.

Therefore, it is for you to decide whether you want play the tricks or you want to ear a long-term reputation. The choice is yours.

Wearing expensive brands and having a costly pair of shoes is not your identity; that is peer pressure. I want you to look beyond clothing labels and create your own brand.

> Whatever you give, you will receive. If you deal with people around you with love and respect, you will get the same back.

It is for you to decide what you want to be known for—your jeans or your genes? The choice is yours.

Do not be the same, be better. (Unknown)

Your character also reflects in your behaviour with others. How you behave with the people around you is really important.

How you maintain your relationships with people and how people look at you is important.

If you're not good to the people around you, then they will never be good to you, and good things will not come to you.

Whatever you give, you will receive. If you deal with people around you with love and respect, you will get the same back.

If you will maintain a distance from the people and not connect with them, the same reaction will come from the other side.

Your world is not limited to yourself; your world has a lot of people attached to it who have an impact on your life.

So be sure of the path you follow and the way you walk because that will affect your final destination. Be a part of the crowd, and be 'alone' in that crowd with your own DNA.

Now, we come back to the basic question: what is your identity? Your identity comes from your basic family values you carry, your passion, and what you do to others.

What you do for yourself and what you do to others cannot go against the basic fabric of society, and you need to create a niche for yourself.

To create your identity, you have to do something extraordinary to stand out in the crowd.

Also, you need to understand the basic difference. Are you a follower and chase somebody's identity, or are you a leader and create your own identity?

My strong advice would be: do not be a shadow of somebody. Stand tall, and create your own shadows.

You are original, do not die as copy. (Unknown)

Simply being born into a nice, good family is no identity for you; that is your family's identity.

What have you created? What have you done in life? What is the thing in your life that carries your signature? That is you. That is your identity.

What have you created? What have you done in life? What is the thing in your life that carries your signature?

If you think that there is nothing that you can pen down now, no big deal. You can start now.

Start working on making your own character, your own brand image, and make sure you put in a good amount of basic ingredients of moral values and character.

Now, you need to spice up your identity with some special flavours, with some special, unique things which you do, and some special personality traits which only you have.

Go on and build a unique, solid identity for yourself, and don't be a shadow of somebody.

It's my life, and I have my own identity.

When you have your own identity, which is clean and identifiable, then all the energy related to that identity are delivered and connected directly to you because the universe has a clear line of command. When you are confused or doing wrong things, the universe also gets mixed signals, and it will be difficult to attract positive energies in your direction.

*It's my life
and I am grateful.*

Chapter 11

It's my life, and I don't owe anything to anybody

'It's my life, and I am what I am because of me. I don't owe anything to anybody.'

'How can I be grateful to anybody if I am not happy?'

'I have not got what I have ever wanted, so I don't believe in any superpower.'

That's the beginning of the problem. We are not thankful for what we have and are always looking for more and more.

If you don't appreciate and respect what you have, how do you expect more blessings to come to you? Many of the teens carry this thankless attitude which does not lead them anywhere.

This is how a typical teen thinks.

'I live in a nice house in a posh locality. I have a servant and a driver. I have my own room with a small television and my own wardrobe. But have I ever been grateful for this?'

'My parents drop me every day for my tuitions and school and also provide me with good food and drinks. I get all the fresh fruits that I love. But have I ever been grateful for this?'

'I get gifts on every festival and special ones on my birthday. I can go shopping with my mum anytime. But have I ever been grateful for this?'

'My family goes for dinners and vacations pretty often, and it's amazing to spend time with my family. But have I ever been grateful for this?'

'My mom makes really good food. Everybody likes to eat my tiffin in school. She makes whatever we tell her to make without hesitation. But have I ever been grateful for this?'

'My friends are always there for me. They are really trustworthy people. Even though we tend to fight a lot, I love them. Have I ever been grateful to them?'

Being grateful is the first step towards happiness. Our thanklessness and being ungrateful close the doors to happiness, and we get locked in where we are.

Welcome to - It's my life, my way

There are so many things that happen in our lives that bring happiness to our lives, but we are never grateful for them.

It's not happiness that brings us gratitude, it's gratitude that brings us happiness. (Unknown)

We already have many things in life, but instead of being thankful and grateful for what we already have, we keep cribbing for more things and remain upset most of the time.

How beautiful it would be if we are happy and grateful for a cup of coffee and then think about cake. How nice it would be if we are grateful for the small car we have and then wish to have a bigger car and so on.

> The root of joy is gratefulness. (David Steindl-Rast)

There are many times when you expect something from life but you don't get that and you get something else.

At that point in time, you crib why you didn't get what you wanted, but you forget to be grateful for what you got instead. We are humans; we have unlimited wants and unlimited desires, but we forget that we also have to have unlimited gratitude.

Simple things like being grateful can have such a great impact on your life that you have no idea about it.

> Be thankful for what you have and you'll end up having more. If you concentrate on what you do not have, you'll never, ever have enough. (Oprah Winfrey)

Let us start with simple things. Do we acknowledge if somebody does anything for us, or do we take it for granted? Yes, we do say thank you sometimes, but actually how many times?

Simple things like being grateful can have a great impact on your life.

Do you say it as many times as you should? Do you say it as much as it's actually needed?

No, you don't. Until and unless you say it about fifty to seventy times a day and for every little thing, it is not done.

Silent gratitude isn't much use to anyone. (Gladys Bronwyn Stern)

If you are not acknowledging the things already delivered to you, how do you accept delivery of more things to you?

Start it now. Do not be a miser here. Give thanks as much as you can.

But before you move ahead, it's time for a task.

The task has to be done for twenty-four hours. Please figure out your twenty-four hours according to your time of reading this.

Now the task is simple easy but still very tough. All you have to do for the next twenty-four hours is you have to say as much thank you as you can and keep a count of it. Like every time you say thank you, just keep counting it. And even when you don't feel it's very important to say thank you, still say it. Every little thanks counts.

For example, if somebody gets a glass of water for you, say thank you, and even when somebody clicks a picture for you, say thank you.

> Feeling gratitude and not expressing it Is like wrapping a present and not giving it. (William Ward)

So now it's your time to you to get up and do the task. Best of luck. Say as much thank you as you can—even if you don't feel like it, even if people around you get annoyed, even if it is not even required. Just be grateful. And obviously, do not proceed to the portion for post—task reading before completing this task.

For post-task reading:

So, dear reader, how do you feel?

How many times did you say thank you? Please don't say ten to twenty times and be proud of yourself because that's too few. Even fifty times wouldn't be too much.

So now, why did I make you do this task? I want you to understand the importance, magnitude, and charisma of gratitude.

I'm sure so many people must have said welcome to you; if not that, they must have smiled at you, and they must have really cherished that moment.

So many people would have felt good about the fact that you said thank you to them for what they did for you. And they would have been glad that out of the ten people they met, at least you were the one who expressed your gratitude.

And I hope you know that you have to do this task every day, like it has to become a daily routine for you, and soon you'll love being grateful.

And also when you're grateful, other people will look at you and become grateful. You'll be making a gratitude chain, which will eventually become a happiness chain. If you break the chain with your sadness and negativity, you're the one at a loss.

Have an attitude of gratitude. (Thomas S. Manson)

Once you learn to become grateful, you'll start feeling so nice and happy, and you start realizing how much people are losing by not being grateful.

Often in our busy lives, we forget to be grateful, but we still give more importance to finding faults. But these small things tend to make big differences in our lives.

Saying thank you is like a gesture of humility. Our Western counterparts learned it since they were born, but it's never too late. By now, I'm sure you would have got the power of gratitude absolutely clear in your mind.

> Happiness is itself a kind of gratitude. (Joseph Wood Krutch)

Gratitude or being grateful is not a difficult job or something that has to be forcefully instilled in you. You might have to do it intentionally for some time, and then it will become a habit. And if it doesn't become a habit for you, I recommend you to do it intentionally.

But you have to be grateful regardless of anything, whatsoever it may be.

Gratitude for what you have is your insurance for future things that you want from this universe. Make a good investment today; invest in gratitude.

It's my life, and I am grateful for what I have.

When you are grateful, you are relaxed and are in the state of receiving and having received things. This is a very positive feeling against the opposite feeling of wanting, lack, and desperation, which are all negative feelings and push your dreams away from you since you are on an opposite frequency. Quite simply, when we are grateful, we are on receiving mode, and when not, we are on a 'shop closed' mode. You choose. So gratitude is your way to the delivery of fresh blessings. Give as much as you can.

It's my life and I live my life fully.

Chapter 12

It's my life, but I have many restrictions

'It's my life, but it is not worth living. There are so many restrictions.'

'I am a grown-up now. I am not a kid any more. Why so many restrictions?'

'I want to fly free in my life. Why can't I do what I want?'

Yes, my teen friends, this is for you guys. You want absolute freedom, a freedom to do the things you want to do. At this sensitive age, you have so many questions as to why you are being exposed to so many barriers.

All youngsters want to live their lives to the full extent, but they always feel somebody is stopping them. Look at how they feel.

'My parents give me the liberty to go out, but they always have a list of so many dos and don'ts. I can't enjoy much. Do I live life fully?'

'I am not a big fan of history class. It's a very serious subject. I can't mug up all the history dates. I would prefer to spend more time on volleyball instead. Do I live life fully?'

'I want to become a singer, but everyone says I won't be able to make enough money. Joining my dad's business will make me earn so much more. Do I live life fully?'

'I want to make all decisions for myself. It becomes an even bigger issue when my parents and I have conflicting views. Do I live life fully?'

This is one of the biggest challenges the teens have—freedom, the freedom to fly. This is where I think we need some more discussion.

Welcome to - It's my life, my way

Are you a free bird? Or are you feeling caged?

If you aren't living 100 per cent, then you'll not be living life; you'll only be chasing life.

You can't be in the swimming pool and not swimming. You can't be in school and not be studying. That's why you can't be alive and not be living fully with the core of your heart.

> To live is the rarest thing in the world, most people exist, that's all. (Oscar Wilde)

When you want to live your life to the fullest extent, you obviously do not want any restrictions; you want to be free. So by being free here, I'm referring to breaking your boundaries and doing something big—doing what you feel like doing, spending time on what you love, chilling with the people you love, and more.

> You only live once, but if you do it right, once is enough. (Mae West)

You shouldn't feel caged at any point in life; only then will you be living a free life. You shouldn't be sitting in a shell and waiting for the egg to hatch; you should be ready to break it on your own.

What is real freedom?

The real freedom is freedom of mind and freedom of thought. Most of the teens have a perception that it is the physical freedom they want, but what I am talking about is the mental freedom.

> The real freedom is freedom of mind and freedom of thought.

You should have your space to grow—yes, a mental space and not a physical space necessarily. You have to discover yourself instead of blaming others. Others are others, not you.

Focus on yourself. Sit alone. Sit still. Do meditation. Do anything to explore yourself.

Talk to yourself; an open heart-to-heart talk with yourself is your real freedom.

> Focus on yourself. Sit alone. Sit still. Do meditation. Do anything to explore yourself.

Take everybody else out; that is your turning point in life. You have made your life so dependent on others' opinions and choices.

Open your own think tank, and see the difference in one week. You will feel free like a lion in the jungle.

Freedom requires that you discover your inner language, your own life rules, your own vision.
(Zephyr Bloch-Jorgensen)

Nobody is stopping you from what you want to do. It is you and you alone who are responsible for your decisions.

More often than not, we feel that others stop us from living our lives 100 per cent. That's a big myth.

Nobody is stopping you from what you want to do. It is you and you alone who are responsible for your decisions.

Many things which may not be good for teens can what about other things?

You have to dig deep into yourself, find out the original you, and then just be yourself as you are.

Does anybody stop you from playing tennis or squash or cricket? Does anybody stop you from singing, playing music, dancing? Does anybody stop you from doing photography, web designing, or even making heritage projects?

It is your willingness or unwillingness that is stopping you. We always find one excuse or other for not doing things, and that is our excuse for our whole lives. We keep it in the file for records.

It's your life. You have to dig deep into yourself, find out the original you, and then just be yourself as you are.

You don't need freedom to be yourself. (Terence Chiew)

Nobody is going to ask you after twenty years, 'Why did you not play tennis if you love it so much?' It's your call; you have to do it today. If you will keep thinking and keep blaming, life will go on, time will slip by, and you would still be waiting.

> I am the one that has to die when it's time for me to die, so let me live my life the way I want to. (Jimi Hendrix)

You should be willing to live the crazy life.

Living the crazy life means living life to the fullest and living each and every moment and making the most of it. Well, there are many folks who waste time on stupid things and forget that each moment has its importance.

> This is your life and it's ending one minute at a time. (*Fight Club*)

This is for those people who focus on the problems and not the priceless value of each moment. They just want to justify why they have not been able to do something. Nobody is interested in listening to excuses.

> I am not afraid of dying, I am afraid I have not been alive enough. (*Mr Nobody*)

If you just sit down once and think about all the times when you could have actually lived life but you lost them in your crying and raising demands, that's when you'll realize how much time you have wasted.

So to live life, it means becoming crazy and enjoying every moment whether you are doing the most boring thing or you're with the best people.

You have to make sure that you do all that you have wanted to do in life because all you can do later is regret.

> **You have to make sure that you do all that you have wanted to do in life because all you can do later is regret.**

Of course, nobody can get you the time back. So you have to be really careful when you're spending time being sad or depressed because all you're doing is letting go of happy moments.

You never know when life will come to an end, and you'll be lying in bed wondering, 'Why didn't I do everything that I wanted to? Why was I so stupid? I could have done so much more.'

However, you won't get another chance then. Thus, it's very important for you to realize the importance of the time you have and make the most it.

Everyone knows how to make excuses for not exploring the full potential, but the happier people are those who create their own freedom. You need to be free from within. You need to live life to the fullest from within and only for yourself.

Life is a continuous journey. The river will keep flowing whether you hop on the boat and flow along with it or just decide to sit at the shore and keep on thinking.

Your friend might just sit on the boat and move ahead and live a wonderful life. But you'll be stuck up there still figuring out what to do.

Others will do what their mind and heart tells them to, but I don't want you to stay at the shore.

So move ahead, step on the boat, and experience the joyous ride. Do everything that makes you go crazy because I don't think you are getting the chance again.

Take life like a roller-coaster ride, a fun-filled journey where we scream, shout, laugh, smile, enjoy, and get scared, and in the end, we will love it.

That's how life is—scary, tough, and sad, yet lovely, amazing, and fantastic. So live with open arms! Live as much as you can because it's your life. It's like your own self.

> Take life like a roller-coaster ride, a fun-filled journey.

The best way to live a happy life is to live with all the freedom and with no boundaries attached.

It's my life, and I live life fully.

When you live your life fully, you directly log on to a higher frequency, which is having more happiness, more energy, and more blessings. The universe responds back to you with a pack of positivity and happiness. On the other hand, if you are living a restricted life with so many terms and conditions, the universe gets a very conditional message, and it cannot give you unlimited supply of happiness and prosperity.

It's my life and I love it.

Chapter 13

It's my life, but I don't love it

'It's my life, but I don't see anything worth loving. My life is a real chaos.'

'I am a good person, but nobody loves me. What should I do?'

'How do you expect me to love my pet when I am not happy on my own?'

Do these statements sound familiar to you? Have you heard any teen talking of the same stuff? I have heard a lot of similar-sounding arguments. We can find thousands of reasons not to give love.

Teens today just want one-sided love. How can you expect somebody to love you if you don't love anybody around you?

Let us check a few examples. Whom do you love?

'My family consists of really good people. I love all of them. But sometimes when they become moody, I start distancing from them. Do I love my family?'

'My friends have always been my support, but we also have so many differences. Sometimes we don't talk for months. That's when I start questioning my love for them. Do I love my friends?'

'We live in a simple flat in the suburbs. But my friends live in farmhouses with four to five cars and multiple helpers. I feel so jealous of them at times. Do I love my house?'

'For my birthdays, I generally get clothes and accessories, but other people in my colony always get new gadgets on their birthdays, and then they tease me. Do I love my material possessions?'

'I'm a little chubby. I want to lose weight, but Mum says this is not the right age for dieting. The other girls in my class are skinner and prettier than me. Do I love myself?'

'My life is okay. Not too good, not too bad. I always wish I could live Bill Gates's life. He lives a perfect life. My life is not like his life. Do I love my life?'

As you see, you will be able to find numerous reasons for not loving the things and situations around you.

It's very easy and almost spontaneous to find faults and find reasons to break something, and we need to really work hard to find reasons to love something, somebody, and everybody.

Welcome to - It's my life, my way

Have you ever loved your life and everything that is a part of your life? Or have you always found the grass greener on the other side?

> Love is when other person's happiness is more important than your own. (H. Jackson Brown Jr)

By loving life, I mean here not loving only one moment or one incident but loving each and every moment of your life.

Love is the greatest possible force; it can change a lot, and it can do wonders. Loving life means loving each day of your life, loving each thing that happens in your life—big or small, good or bad.

If you make up your mind with 'Yes, I have to love everything, everyone, every place, every event of my life,' you will start loving them in no time. And once you start loving, you will realize the potential of love in your life.

> You never lose by loving. You always lose by holding back. (Barbara De Angelis)

Love is the greatest possible force; it can change a lot, and it can do wonders.

Love is not just the love between a husband and wife, a girlfriend and boyfriend, or for that matter, the love between a mother and son or a father and daughter. Love is a much greater force.

Love is all around you; it is your love for your new car, your house, your clothes, your favourite topic, your phone, your friends, your idol, your ambition, and so much more.

Surely, your love for these things can give you so much that you cannot even imagine. You can get all the things that you wish for and are attracted to just by loving them exclusively.

And how does this happen?

Well, once you love them, you will automatically start thinking about them, then you will start talking about them then and imagining yourselves with the things you love, and in no time, they will be yours.

Faith makes all things possible . . . love makes all things easy. (Dwight L. Moody)

But on the other hand, there might be things in your life which you are not attracted to or which you dislike. Does that mean you start hating them?

You simply should just ignore the things you don't like and move ahead. Please do not react to the things you do not like. Leave them as they are.

If you focus only on the things you love and desire in your life, life not only becomes like a cakewalk, but you also save up on a lot of time which would have only been wasted on negative people and unwanted things.

The things that make you happy and give you positive feelings are those which should be kept in your heart and mind all the time.

When heart is open, the present moment Is more than enough. When heart is closed it's never enough. (Michael Jeffreys)

Those things which make you sad, which fail to attract your attention, and which give you negative feelings, should never be kept in your heart and mind.

It is very important to know what you do love or what you do want and to focus only on them.

It is very important to know what you do love or what you do want and to focus only on them.

Let me give you an example of my life. I have always loved dancing, and it is something which has always given me immense happiness and joy. With God's blessings, I was promoted to a higher batch in Shiamak Davar's Institute for the Performing Arts.

I continued working hard as a dancer, wanting to be promoted to the highest batch in New Delhi (the special-potential batch). I kept dreaming about it and wrote down: 'I want to be in SPB.' I proved myself as a dancer, and believe it or not, last year in July, I was promoted to the special-potential batch. I was on cloud nine!

This is just because I was clear in my head that dance is my passion and that I love it more than any other activity and because I kept on loving it more and more each day and said that, yes, I want to be in SPB that I got in there.

Now on the other hand, let me give you another example. One day I was going for my dance class, and I got a little late in leaving. And on my way, I was just saying, 'I don't want to be late for class! I don't.' And guess what? I was fifteen minutes late for class, and I even got a scolding.

On the contrary, the next time I was a little late for class, I started saying, 'I want to reach on time. I want to reach on time.' And guess what? When I reached the class, everyone was standing outside. The previous class had been extended, and I still had five more minutes.

Trust me, I'm not even kidding. This actually works! I'm telling you, I tried both of these things. Initially, even I didn't believe in all this, but when I actually started doing this, I realized, 'Oh my god, this actually works.'

So learn to love; in fact, love is something that each one of us knows how to do; you just have to find the right things to love and then let the magic of love do wonders.

> I have found that if you love life, life will love you back.
> (Arthur Rubinstein)

That's because once you start loving everything in your life—from the traffic on your way to the mall to buying your favourite dress, from standing in the queue in the food court to getting your favourite food—life becomes so easy and simple.

You just have to find the right things to love and then let the magic of love do wonders.

But the problem that most of you face is that, you tend to focus more on those things which you don't love than on those which you love, or those things which you don't want than on the things which you want and love.

 That's when the greatest force, love, fails to make your life marvellous; it's because you are so busy in the issues of your life that you tend to forget that these things are pointless in your life. That's when you have more of negativity than more of love. It does not take you anywhere.

You can love anything, provided you want it, and that could be anything from loving your stuffed toy to loving your life partner.

And you don't have to bother if anybody else has a different opinion about it.

But yes, while you keep loving and doing what you want, you have to give equal respect and regard to others' opinions and thoughts. For them, it is their prime love. Give them their space. Do not fight over that.

You may love something so badly that you start hating others because they do not love what you love. That's a big disaster you are heading to.

Love also plays a very important role in relationships. The foundation of every relationship is love. Surely there are other factors, such as understanding, trust, etc., but no relationship can exist without love and bonding.

Love also plays a very important role in relationships. The base of every relationship is love.

Don't rely on someone else for your happiness and self-worth. Only you can responsible for it. You have to invest in yourself, or no one else will. (Stacey Charter)

Any relationship—whether one between a girl and a boy, brother and sister, or mother and son—all of them survive on love.

Therefore, your lack of love or your abundance of love for someone can make or break your

relationships. Love in a relationship means loving the other person and not finding faults in them.

Once you start loving others as they are, they will start loving you for what you are.

Once you start loving others as they are, they will start loving you for what you are.

But before that, you need to love yourself. Just like you need to love your life and every aspect of it, you need to love everything about yourself. You need to love your hair, your nose, your skin—everything.

To be loved, be lovable. (Ovid)

So love cannot be for only one particular thing/person/event in your life. Love has to be universal.

Love has no boundaries, no limits; you can love anything, anytime, anywhere. Love has no limits; you can love as much as possible.

Love has no boundaries, no limits; you can love anything, anytime, anywhere.

Never love for the sake of loving, or do not love something or someone more than others.

Love cannot be judgemental. It does not know how to be biased; it is not conditional and is without opinions.

Love has no limits; you can love as much as possible.

Love the life you live. Live the life you love. (Bob Marley)

Only you know what to love, whom to love, how much to love. Only you have the power to do so because you love.

So love your life. Love everything and everybody every time, without even thinking twice.

It's my life, and I love life.

Love is the highest frequency of your being. But there is no limit on how much you can love. Love is limitless. When you are in love with this universe, the universe will love you too. When you love somebody, something, some place, you are getting connected to the main terminal; you become part of the bigger circuit. Now imagine, if you love everything and everybody all around, you are getting connected to the bigger community every time, and slowly you become invincible because you love this world.

The Final Word

*It's my life and
I am flying.*

It's my life, and I am ready to take off

We all want to be happy. We all want to be successful, but everyone has issues. We all have big dreams, and we all have a long list of problems.

The objective here is to overcome the problems and chase your dreams. You have to cut the noise which distracts you, and you need to bring the focus back on achieving your goals.

The reason behind writing this book was that I could feel that you go through a lot of peer pressure and expectations, but there is no guidance available for you to have an amazing life.

This is neither fiction nor a book on philosophy of life; it is a call to action. This book aims to stir your soul and hit your conscience for you to come out of the day-to-day teenage trauma in which you are stuck.

Let us recap what we all have discussed so far.

Happiness

Teenage life is full of desires and expectations, which are accompanied by problems and obstacles. We all want to be happy; that is where the problem starts. We want to be happy, but we are not happy now.

When we are happy, happy things come to us. We feel more elevated, and we get better and better results. One thing leads to another, and that is what I call the *chain of happiness.*

Change

But the issue here is how we start the chain, how to be happy first when we have all the problems around us. The common explanation is that there are so many issues, and nothing can be done as if it is the end of the tunnel.

That is where our story starts. The first thing we need to admit and acknowledge is that there is nothing fixed in life and life can change. Change is life. Life changes. That is why opportunities come.

Nothing is constant in life, and we all go through the change. Whether we like it or not, changes will happen. The earlier we accept it, the better it will be.

Now the next point for you is to change yourself. You are not frozen in stone; you also have to change. You have to change and adapt to the changing situations, circumstances, and needs.

Once you understand and accept this—that change is a must—and you are ready to change, half of the battle is won. Now let us move to the next.

Acceptance

The next thing in life is to learn the art of acceptance. You need to learn to accept the things as they are—everybody and everything every time.

Accept the reality; accept your parents, family, neighbourhood, and the strings attached. Life is a package; you do not get to pick and choose options everywhere.

If we keep busy in criticism, blames, excuses, and justifications, we will not get any headway in life. You have to take a deep breath now and accept everything as it is.

accept you as you are. There will be no fuss around, and you will be in harmony with the universe, ready to move to the next level.

Self-belief

Now you are happy, and you are ready to change. You accept the change, and you are accepting everything around you. So we come back to you.

Do you believe in yourself? Do you believe that the dreams, goals, and targets you have planned for yourself are yours? Do you think you have all the skills and knowledge to take you to the top, or are you unsure about yourself?

Most of us are victims of self-guilt, self-criticism, and to an extent, self-pity. If you do not love and respect yourself, nobody will respect you. On the contrary, if you believe in yourself, the whole world will believe in you.

You may occasionally develop negative feelings of self-doubt. You have to trash this out immediately, and you have to inculcate the feelings of self-belief and courage and confidence to deliver the results.

Our faith in ourselves promotes our faith in the universe. We all come in sync with one another, and the universe will be ready to shower its blessings.

Appreciation

Many times, you are busy finding faults and are not able to appreciate the good points in a particular situation.

As a next step in life, you have to learn to appreciate the beauty of life around you as you get and learn to respect the efforts done by others. If you do, others will appreciate your efforts and you.

It is all give and take. You get what you give. You appreciate people; people will appreciate you. You criticize people; they will criticize you.

The rule of the game is, never ever criticize anybody, and learn to appreciate everything everywhere and every time.

Problems

However, our biggest concern is the problems that stop us from accepting and appreciating life. Actually, the problems aren't that big a deal if we focus on the solutions.

So long as you keep discussing the problems, the problems will keep increasing. You need to shift the focus to solutions.

The moment you stop discussing the problems and start thinking about the solutions, you start getting out of the problem.

Problems are like small hurdles on your way, which you have to solve to reach to the finishing line. Once you cross the big hurdles, you get more experience, and you become more confident.

Passion

Passion is what you are made of; that is your inner being. If you follow your passion, your journey to success will be effortless. You will shine like a star, and success will be granted.

Once you do something which you are passionate about, every part of your body and every cell in your body will excel to perform the best, and the results are nothing less than a miracle.

Your passion has to be complemented with your dedication, sincerity, hard work, and commitment to get the desired results. The second most important ingredients of success are your courage and willpower.

Thoughts and feelings

This is actually the starting point. Good feelings and good thoughts lead to a better, happier life, and you will attract happy people and get happy circumstances in your way.

Our thoughts and feelings are the guiding lines for our destiny. We can control our thoughts and our feelings and decide how we react to a particular situation or event.

Whatever we think about, we bring about.

By consistently thinking and feeling about our goals, we can turn the waves of fortune in our direction and then, in a way, create our little world.

The process of visualization of your dreams, which is a scientifically proven concept, is also an extension of the process of thoughts and feelings.

Character

Your passion gives you identity, but that identity has to be coupled with ethics and your moral values with which you deal with the outside world.

Your basic character and integrity is going to go a long way in achieving your goals than the shortcuts you may try here and there.

You might have all the money in the world, but you will never get all the reputation and appreciation without a good, credible image.

Gratitude

Most of the time, we keep getting things we have been asking for, and sometimes even without asking, our parents give it to us as part of their blessings.

How many times do you feel grateful for the things you already have? Or do you rather always keep cribbing for the things you don't have?

If you do not acknowledge the receipt of the things you already have, how do you expect the universe to deliver you more?

You have to make this a habit—being grateful and being thankful for your pipeline of blessings to continue.

Freedom

Some of us may be living a life full of restrictions and boundaries, but they'll be regretting that later in their life. Thus, the best way to live your life is to enjoy and cherish each and every moment.

The point here is that all of us without exception blame others for caging us and putting restrictions on our lives.

The fact of the matter is that we ourselves are responsible for our lives and we need to take responsibility of both our actions and inactions.

There are limitations in life, but you have to learn to live life fully, 100 per cent, in order to achieve great heights.

Love

It is one world, and we are all connected though the binding force of love. Love connects all families, friends, couples, siblings, societies, races, and even countries.

The day we start loving our neighbours, our friends, and everybody around us, we are opening the doors to heaven. Love has no boundaries and no limits.

We can and should love everything, everybody, and under every situation. This is one common thread which will take you places, flying high against the gravity.

You just need to love the things you love and desire and to keep your love pure and clean. A clean love for the right things will always give you wonderful results.

With all the new tips that you have learned in this book, you will automatically start loving your life, and once you love your life, nothing will seem out of place to you. Your life will become beautiful.

All the successful people in the world have followed these simple rules and made their lives marvellous; it is now time for you to make your life amazing.

At this tender age of being a teen, you may have lots of doubts, fears, and queries, but if you conquer these now, you will live a fantastic life for the rest of your years.

We've all got only one life, and we all want to make the most of this life. We are unlimited beings.

A king has to win many small battles before he is finally crowned. However, he gains and loses a lot during those small battles.

Right now, it may seem like a long and lengthy process that has unlikely consequences, but once you start following it, it will seem like an easy process.

Your dreams won't seem too far, and they will turn into reality before you even know it.

Others will still be busy complaining about their lives, but you would have already made it to the top.

These tips are not too tough and complicated, nor are these very easy and basic; they need your patience and cooperation.

The master key is with you; you just need to take it out of your pocket, open the door, and receive the treasure. If you get distracted by the surroundings, then you will miss the door.

So you need to simply follow all the tips given in this book. Please do not just read them and forget about them; you have to perform.

You have to act; you have to get out of your bed and deliver. You have to come out of your comfort zone if you want to follow your dreams.

You cannot be sitting on the fence and waiting for the things to fall on your lap. You have to try, try, and keep trying till you succeed in the end.

The biggest failure would be not having tried the things and getting scared of the results. To be successful, you need a lot of courage and conviction. You need to follow your intuition and face the music as it comes.

Just keep moving. Don't stop. Walk ahead with all that comes. The treasure isn't too far.

You already have the boarding pass. You just need to get to the security check and boarding gate, and your flight is ready to take you to your destination.

You just need to be ready to fly, be ready to reach your destination with all your energy, enthusiasm, and drive.

It's my life, and I am flying.